D1651368

THE STORY OF
HOPE

Kids

Discovering the Provision in God's Plan

Free Leader's Guide: www.GoodSoil.com/free

THE STORY OF HOPE

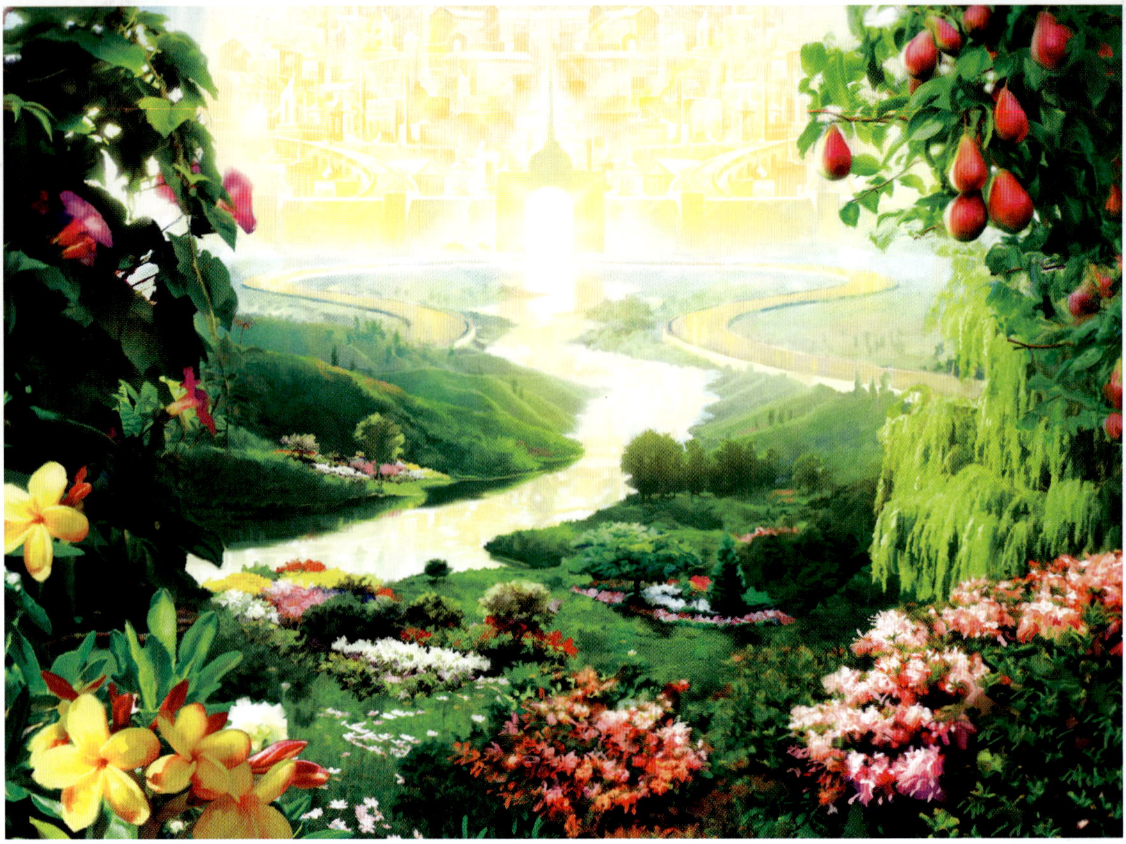

Discovering the Provision in God's Plan

2017 Edition

© 2013 Good Soil Evangelism & Discipleship

Association of Baptists for World Evangelism
P.O. Box 8585
Harrisburg, PA 17105 USA
Phone: (877) 959-2293

980 Adelaide Street South, Suite 34
London, Ontario N6E 1R3 CANADA
Phone: (877) 690-1009

Story Art: Justinen Creative Group

Graphic Design: Justinen Creative Group
& Miriam Ritchie Design

Authors: Wayne Haston, Ron Berrus &
Karen Weitzel

ISBN 978-1-888796-49-0 (Trade Paper)

All rights reserved. No portion of this book may be reproduced in any form without the written permission of the publisher.

All Scripture quotations are taken from the New King James Version® (NKJV®) of the Bible (Thomas Nelson, Inc.).

Printed in the United States of America.

Email: Info@GoodSoil.com
Web: www.GoodSoil.com

CONTENTS

DID YOU KNOW?

The Bible is the most amazing book ever written! It is actually 66 books in one book. God directed 40 men to write the Bible over a period of more than 1,500 years. These authors lived at different times and in different places. They came from different backgrounds and occupations. Some were kings, some were fishermen, one was a doctor, others were prophets. Parts of the Bible were written in three different languages on three continents.

The Bible is different from all other books.

Do you like stories? The Bible has more than 500 stories with almost 3,000 people! But from the beginning of the Bible, one Big Story is woven throughout each book like a thread through a piece of cloth.

The Big Story captures your attention from the very beginning. You want to keep reading because the plot is so intriguing. You soon find out there is one interesting main person and lots of fascinating men and women in the stories. Along the way many mysteries are uncovered, and at the end of the story there is a dramatic ending.

The Big Story begins wonderfully, goes terribly wrong, but ends better than you could have imagined. You should read the Bible, especially if you have never read it. Even if you think you know what it says, or you are skeptical about the Bible because of what others have said, you need to read it for yourself.

▶ The Bible is a best seller in many countries.

People who read the Bible know why it is popular. After the Big Story went terribly wrong, people everywhere had a great need. The Bible tells about God's wonderful and unique provision that takes care of this need and brings eternal hope to people of all times and places.

▶ The Bible contains God's story of hope.

If you want to understand the Bible, it is best to study it from the beginning to the end. This Bible study book will help you to do just that.

All of the Bible's stories are true stories.

HOW TO USE THIS BOOK

There are 40 stories in this book on pages 12 to 51. Start with the first one and read each in order. There are three ways to read the stories:

1. You can read through this book by reading just the key sentence in each colored box for all 40 stories.

2. You can read a couple of stories at a time by reading the key sentence and also the Bible reference(s).

3. You can read one story at a time by reading the key sentence, the Bible reference(s), and then reading and answering the study questions that are listed.

Think of the Bible's Big Story as a mystery. Look for clues that uncover the plot. The plot is what is happening in the story and what will happen. Watch how problems are resolved, how people change, and how promises come true.

Read the word(s) at the bottom of each page. How does the word describe what you learned about God on that page (in the Old Testament section)? How does the word describe what you learned about Jesus (in the New Testament section)?

 The maps on pages 7-9 will help you see where the Bible stories took place.

 The picture of the tabernacle on page 10 will help you to understand how people, who sought God in the early part of the Bible, found hope.

The Bridge to Life is found on pages 52-60. The eight key words that form the bridge come from the Bible's Big Story. Read these pages after you have read through all 40 stories.

Write down any questions. They may be answered as you read through this book. Or ask someone who knows the Bible well.

MAP THE JOURNEY

Maps are fun to use!
Try the activities on this page with the two maps on pages 7-9.

⭐ ### I Live Here
Look at the world map to the right. Do you know where you live? If so, draw a star in the area where you live. If not, ask an adult to help you.

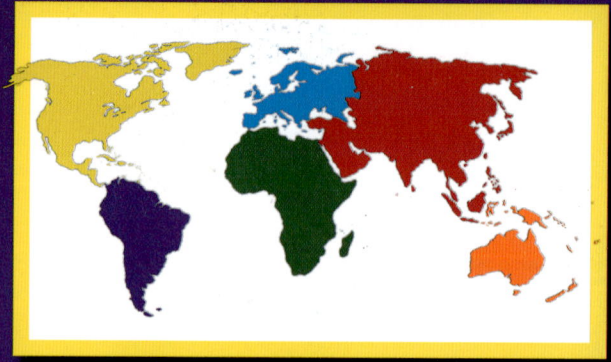

▶ ## Use the Maps for Individual and Team Activities

Individual Activities

🌐 **1. Find the Globe.**
When you see this globe beside an event in this booklet, it means you can find where that event took place on one of the maps. Look on the map(s) and find the area or city mentioned in that event.

2. Trace the Journey.
Throughout the story of hope, God's people traveled from place to place. As you read the events in this booklet, find the areas or cities mentioned on the map(s) and then draw a line from the first location to the next, and the next, and so on.

3. Picture It!
If you like to draw, and even if you don't, you can draw simple pictures on the maps to remind you of what happened at different places. You'll be told when and where to draw a picture. The pictures you draw will be easy, just like the star you drew on the above map.

Team Activities

1. Can You Find It?
If you are using this booklet with more than one person, try this activity together. Turn to one of the maps. One person calls out the name of a place on the map and the others try to find it as quickly as possible. Take turns calling out map names.

2. What Happened There?
Use this activity if you are using this booklet with more than one person.

- Look at the map(s), point to a place, and tell what happened there.

- Chose someone to act out what happened at a particular place (that person chooses the place). The rest of the group must guess what is being acted out and then point on the map to where it took place.

3. If I Could, I'd Go to …
Point to a place on the map and tell why you'd like to go to that place.

Download a Free Leader's Guide: www.GoodSoil.com/TSOH-Kids

WHERE THE STORY TOOK PLACE

The Holy Land
Canaan/Palestine

The Bible is a true story about real people, places, and events. The events happened long ago on earth.

Much of this story of hope took place in the Middle East pictured on this map. We call this area today the Holy Land, but in early Bible times it was called Canaan, and later became known as Palestine.

This is a small area, about 150 miles (240 km) from north to south and 75 miles (120 km) from east to west. The events that happened here many centuries ago still give us hope today.

The Great Sea
(Mediterranean)

Egypt

▲ Mt. Lebanon

Syria

• Tyre

Capernaum • • Bethsaida

Galilee

• Nazareth

Sea of Galilee

Jordan River

Samaria

Shechem • • Sychar

Judah

Jericho •

Mt. Moriah
Jerusalem ▲▲ Mt. of Olives

Bethlehem • • Bethany

Dead Sea

N
W E
S

Edom

The map of the Holy Land on page 7 was where the most important events in *The Story of Hope* took place. The map of the Ancient Near East on these pages is where many other Bible events happened. This area of the world is now called the Middle East. The area in green, from Canaan to Chaldea, has been called the Fertile Crescent because the land there is usable for growing crops.

Haran

The Great Sea (Mediterranean)

Shechem

Jerusalem

Sea of Galilee

Jordan River

Canaan

Dead Sea

Kadesh-barnea

Goshen

Wilderness of Sinai

Edom

Pi Hahiroth

Egypt

Mt. Sinai (Horeb)

Nile River

Red Sea

N

W

E

S

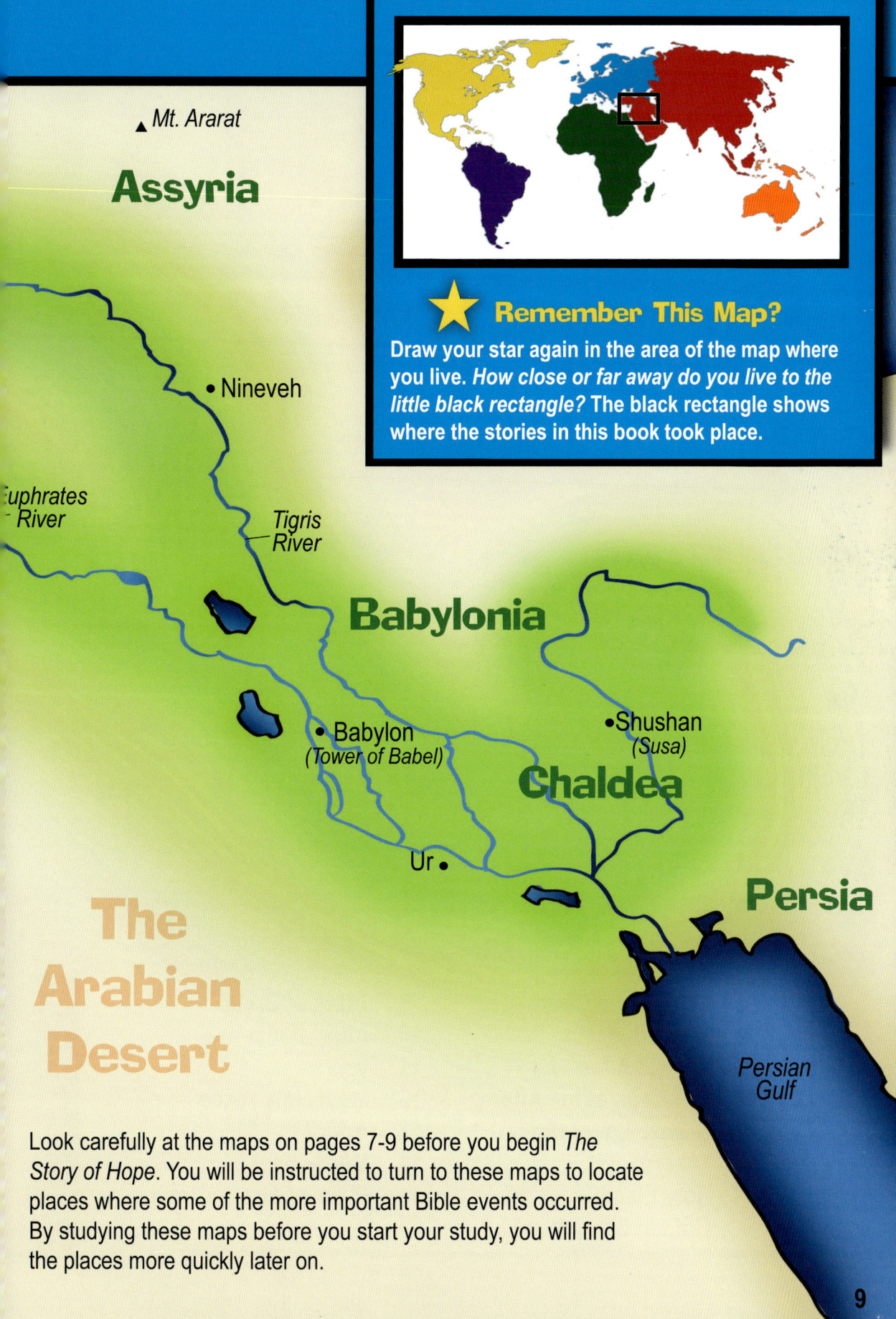

▲ Mt. Ararat

Assyria

• Nineveh

Euphrates River

Tigris River

Babylonia

• Babylon
(Tower of Babel)

•Shushan
(Susa)

Chaldea

Ur •

The Arabian Desert

Persia

Persian Gulf

⭐ **Remember This Map?**

Draw your star again in the area of the map where you live. *How close or far away do you live to the little black rectangle?* The black rectangle shows where the stories in this book took place.

Look carefully at the maps on pages 7-9 before you begin *The Story of Hope*. You will be instructed to turn to these maps to locate places where some of the more important Bible events occurred. By studying these maps before you start your study, you will find the places more quickly later on.

THE TABERNACLE

This unusual structure has an important purpose in the first half of *The Story of Hope*.

You will be instructed when to turn to this page. You will learn why and how this movable tabernacle became a symbol of hope and promise for many people long ago who were seeking God.

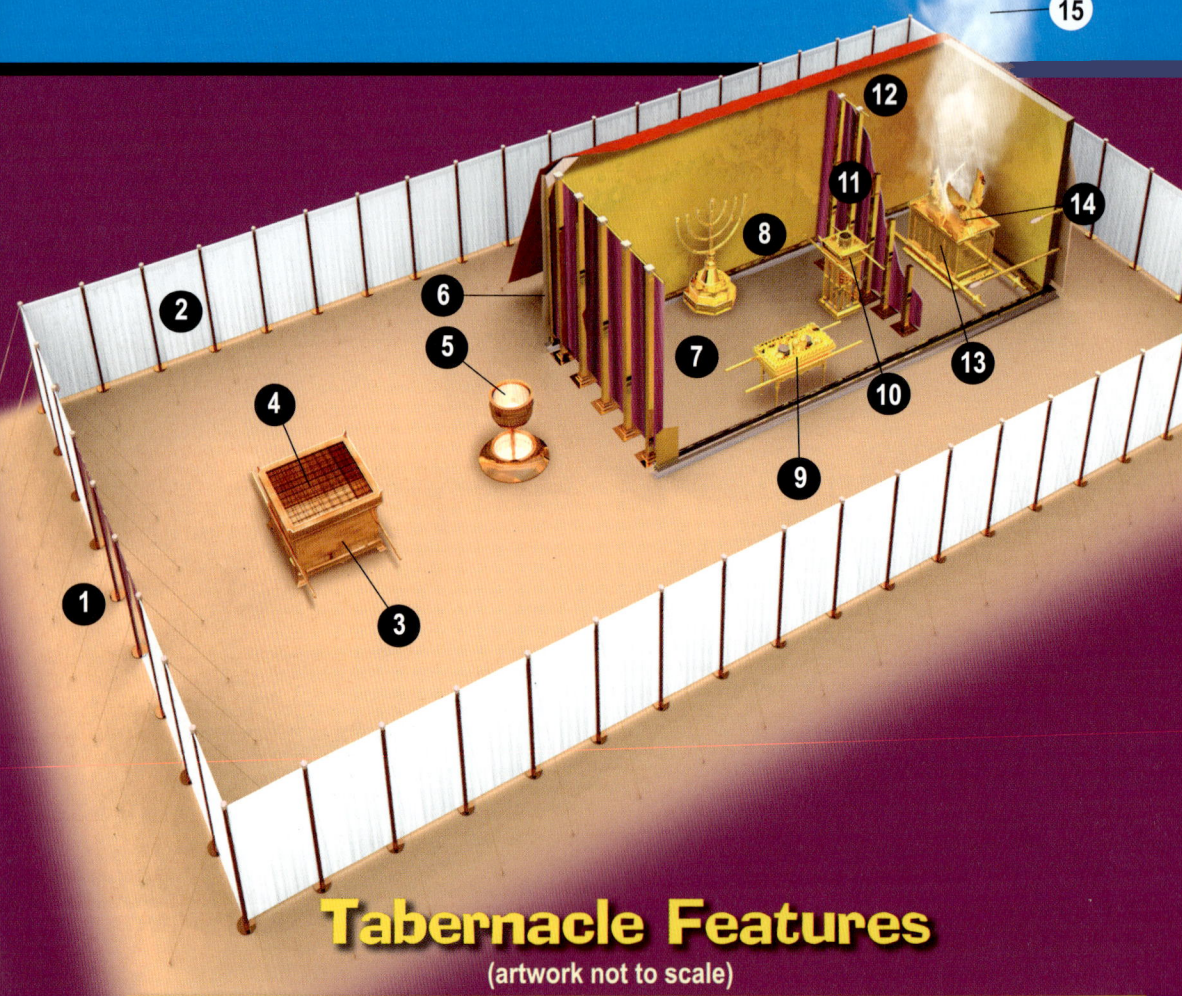

Tabernacle Features
(artwork not to scale)

1. Gate of the Court	9. Table of Bread
2. Court Fence	10. Altar of Incense
3. Bronze Altar	11. Veil
4. Offerings at the Altar	12. Most Holy Place
5. Bronze Laver (Basin)	13. Ark of the Covenant
6. Tabernacle	14. Mercy Seat
7. Holy Place	15. Pillar of Fire & Cloud
8. Golden Lampstand	

THE STORY OF
HOPE
Kids

On the next page, you will begin learning about God's plan for the universe, the spirit world, and the human race. You will learn the answer to questions that men and women of all times and places have asked: How did I get here? What is the meaning of life? What does this life mean to me? What happens after death? How can I be prepared to die?

Turn the page. Begin your experience now with the true, unfolding drama of *The Story of Hope.*

The Eternal God

1

Genesis 1:1
The first sentence in the Bible says that there is a God and that He has always existed.

In the beginning God ...

1. **Read Genesis 1:1.** Does this verse say there is one God or more than one god?

2. **Which statement is true?**

⬭ *The Bible begins by trying to prove that God exists.*

⬭ *The Bible begins by saying that before anything at all was created, God already existed.*

3. **Read Psalm 90:2.** Everlasting or eternal means no beginning and no ending. What does this verse tell us about God?

4. **As you read** through the stories of the Bible, you will learn more about God. You will learn who He is and what He is like.

5. **In the picture** is the Hebrew word for God. It is the word "Elohim" and means the "Strong One."

ACTIVITY
At the bottom of pages 12 to 32 are words that describe God. For each page, read the questions about that event and study the picture. From what you have learned, tell why the name (or names) at the bottom of each page describe God.

Tell why this name describes God:
Eternal Being

Creation of the Universe

2

Genesis 1:1-25

The Bible says God created the universe, including our earth and its heavens. God also created plants and animals.

1. **Creation—Day 1.** Read verses 1-5.
- What was the earth like (verse 2)?
- What did God do in verses 3-5?

2. **Day 2.** Read verses 6-8. What did God divide on this day?

3. **Day 3.** Read verses 9-13.
- What happened first on Day 3 (verses 9-10)?
- What happened next on Day 3 (verses 11-13)?

4. **Day 4.** Read verses 14-19. Why did God put lights in the heavens above the earth?

5. **Day 5.** Read verses 20-23. What animals were created on this day?

6. **Day 6, part 1.** Read verses 24-25. What animals were created on this day?

Tell why this name describes God:
Eternal Being

Creation of Human Beings

3

Genesis 1:26-31; 2:7-25

Then God created a man and a woman, Adam and Eve. God told them to rule over all on earth and not eat fruit from a certain tree.

1. **Day 6, part 2.** Read Genesis 1:26-27. When you compare the creation of man and woman with other creatures, what was special about the creation of human beings?

2. **Read Genesis 1:28-31.** What job did God give Adam and Eve that was not given to other creatures?

3. **Read Genesis 2:7.** What does this verse tell you about the creation of Adam?

4. **Read Genesis 2:8-9.** *True or False? Circle one.*

   The Garden of Eden was a beautiful and fruitful garden.

5. **Read Genesis 2:15-17.** What one thing did God tell Adam not to do? If Adam disobeyed, what would happen?

6. **Read Genesis 2:18-25.** *True or False? Circle one.*

   At this time, there was no reason for Adam and Eve to feel any shame.

Tell why these names describe God:
Almighty Creator   Supreme Authority

Lucifer Falls from Heaven

4

**Ezekiel 28:11-17;
Isaiah 14:12-15**

Lucifer had been a beautiful angel, but led other angels to rebel against God. Lucifer became known as Satan, the Devil.

1. **Angels are spirit beings** that God created to worship and serve Him.

2. **Ezekiel and Isaiah tell about Lucifer's fall from Heaven.** They compare him to the kings of Tyre and Babylon.

   ▪ Read Ezekiel 28:11-17. What was Lucifer like in Heaven?

   ▪ Read Isaiah 14:12-15. What did Lucifer do that caused him to be thrown out of Heaven?

   What did God say would happen to him?

3. **Read Matthew 25:41 and Isaiah 14:15.**
   ◼ Where will Lucifer, or the "Devil," be sent?

   ◼ Who are the Devil's angels?

4. **We do not know when Lucifer rebelled against God.** It happened before the next event and could have happened much earlier.

Tell why these names describe God:
Holy God   Supreme Authority

Beginning of Human Sin

5

Genesis 3:1-6

God loved Adam and Eve. He said: "Do not eat from the forbidden tree." Satan defied God and tempted Eve. She ate and caused Adam to eat.

1. These words are found in the last book of the Bible:

"That old serpent, who is the Devil, or Satan" (Revelation 20:2).

2. Read Genesis 3:1-5. Satan appeared to Eve as a serpent.

- *True or False? Circle one.*

Satan changed God's words and made God seem unloving (compare Genesis 2:16-17 and Genesis 3:1).

- *True or False? Circle one.*

Satan said God would not punish disobedience as He said (see verse 4).

3. Read Genesis 3:6. What three features about the fruit made Eve want to eat what God had forbidden?

4. As you read the Bible, you will learn that to disobey what God commands is "sin."

Tell why these names describe God:
Holy God   Loving Father

6

Genesis 3:7-13; 5:5

God is holy and judges fairly. When Adam and Eve disobeyed, they immediately experienced the result of their sin: separation from God.

1. **"Death" means separation.** Sin causes three kinds of death:
   - spiritual (separation from God)
   - physical
   - eternal

2. **Read Genesis 3:7-13.** After Adam and Eve sinned, they were separated from God. This is called spiritual death.
   - verse 7—they knew they were naked
   - verse 8—they tried to hide from God
   - verses 12-13—they made excuses for their sin and blamed others

3. **Read Genesis 5:5.** What other punishment did Adam receive for his sin?

4. **Read Genesis 5:8, 11, 14, 17, 20, 27, and 31.** Then read Romans 5:12. Adam's disobedience affected all of us in two ways. What are the two ways?

Tell why this name describes God:
Just Judge

Genesis 3:14-15
God promised that one day a special descendant of Eve would defeat Satan.

1. **Read Genesis 3:14.** What changes did God make to the serpent-animal?

2. **Read Genesis 3:15.** Check the correct sentence.

☐ God wanted to cause hatred between people and snakes.

☐ No, something more important was happening here.

3. **The "offspring" of the woman** (a descendant—one born in the same family line, but a long time later) will: *(check all that are true)*

☐ Be a human being

☐ Damage an important part of the serpent's body

☐ Suffer less serious harm in the process of defeating the serpent

4. **This person will be** the offspring (descendant) of the woman, not a man.

Tell why these names describe God:
Loving Father   Kind Protector

8

Genesis 3:7, 21

Adam and Eve tried to cover their guilt and shame with fig leaves. God replaced the leaves with clothing He made from animal skins.

1. Read Genesis 3:7.

- Who made the coverings (clothes) in this verse?

- What kind of covering did they use?

2. Read Genesis 3:21.

- Who made the coverings (clothes) in this verse?

- What kind of covering did He use?

3. **True or False?** *Circle one.*

> *What God did for Adam and Eve showed they had lost their innocence forever. They would always be guilty of sin.*

4. **True or False?** *Circle one.*

> *Because of Adam and Eve's sin, God needed to kill one or more innocent (blameless) animals to prepare coverings for them.*

Tell why these names describe God:
Loving Father   Kind Protector

Expelled from Eden

9

Genesis 3:22-24

God made Adam and Eve leave Eden after they disobeyed Him. They lost their privilege to live in the beautiful garden.

1. Read the first part of Genesis 3:22. *True or False? Circle one.*

> *Because Adam and Eve ate fruit from the forbidden tree, they now had knowledge of evil because of what they had done.*

If this sentence is true, how is Adam and Eve's knowledge of evil different from God's knowledge of evil?

2. Read the second part of Genesis 3:22 through Genesis 3:24.

- **Fact 1:** God expelled Adam and Eve from the Garden of Eden.

- **Fact 2:** the second part of verse 22 tells why God expelled them.

3. Adam and Eve were expelled from Eden as a result of their sin. It was an act of God's judgment. It was also a gracious act. Why? Read the end of verse 22 again.

Tell why these names describe God:
Just Judge   Kind Protector

The Great Flood

10

Genesis 6:5—8:22

Over time, the human race grew and became so sinful God destroyed the earth and everyone with a flood, except for godly Noah and his family.

1. **Read Genesis 6:5-7, 11-12.**
- Why did God send the flood?
- How serious was the problem that caused the flood?

2. **Read Genesis 6:8-10 and 7:1.**
- How was Noah different from the other people?
- "Noah walked with God." What does this sentence mean?

3. **Read Genesis 6:5—8:22.** What kind of flood did God send? Check one box.
- ⬭ a local flood   ⬭ a worldwide flood

4. **Read Genesis 6:15.** How large was the ark?

5. **From this story …**
- What do we learn about the people who lived on the earth?
- What do we learn about God?

Tell why these names describe God:
Just Judge   Kind Protector

11 Promises to Abraham

Genesis 11:31—12:7

Years after the flood, God called Abraham to be the father of a large nation. Through him, all people would receive a spiritual blessing.

 1. **Read Genesis 11:31-32.** Find Ur, Haran, and Canaan on the map on pages 8 and 9.

2. **Read Genesis 12:1-3.** At the end of verse 3 God made one special promise:

All families of the earth will be blessed through Abraham.

This promise is repeated several times in the Bible so it is very important. How could this promise happen? To learn the answer to this question, you will need to wait and see how the Bible's story of hope develops.

3. **Read Genesis 12:4-7.** What additional promise did God give to Abraham in verse 7?

 **ACTIVITY**
On pages 8 and 9, draw a line from Ur to Haran and then draw a line from Haran to Canaan. This is the route Abraham took as God directed him.

Tell why this name describes God:
Faithful Promise Keeper

12

Genesis 22:1-18

God would send the spiritual blessing through Abraham's son, Isaac. God tested Abraham's faith: He asked him to kill his son, but at the last minute He sent a substitute sacrifice.

1. **Read Genesis 22:1-14.**

   ■ Why did God ask Abraham to sacrifice his son?

   ■ Why did Abraham obey this unusual command?

   ■ **Read verse 5 and Hebrews 11:17-19.**

      What did Abraham believe God could do?

   ■ **Read Genesis 22:7-14.**

      How did Abraham show his faith?

2. **Read Genesis 22:15-18.** The special blessing would come through Abraham's offspring.

3. **Later Isaac had a son named Jacob** (God renamed him Israel). Jacob (Israel) had 12 sons. As Israel was preparing to die, what promise did he make to his son, Judah, in Genesis 49:10? A scepter is a staff held by a king that shows his royal authority.

Tell why these names describe God:
Supreme Authority   All-Knowing One

13 Moses Called to Be a Leader

Exodus 1:1-14; 3:1-17

Some of Abraham's descendants (the Israelites) became slaves in Egypt. God called Moses to lead them out of Egypt into Canaan, the land God promised to Abraham.

1. **God directed events** in Israel's family so that his son, Joseph, became a widely known leader in Egypt. God did this to prepare the way for Israel's family to go to Egypt.

2. **Read Exodus 1:1-7.** What happened to Israel's sons and their families?

3. **Read Exodus 1:8-14.** A new Egyptian Pharaoh (king) came to power who did not remember Joseph or the promises made to him. What happened then?

4. **Read Exodus 3:1-10.** What did God want Moses to do? What special relationship did God have with the Israelites?

5. **Read Exodus 3:11-17.** What was Moses supposed to tell the Israelites when they asked "Who sent you?"

   ▪ What did God say in verse 14?

   ▪ What did God say in verse 15?

ACTIVITY
Map: page 8. Draw a burning bush near Mt. Sinai (Horeb).

Tell why this name describes God:
Person to Whom You Can Relate

14 The Plagues and Passover

Exodus 12:1-13, 21-23

To free the Israelites, God sent 10 plagues on Egypt. The last plague caused the death of the firstborn child in every family. God protected those who showed faith in Him.

1. **God sent 10 terrible plagues** to show His power over the false gods of Egypt and to convince Pharaoh to release the Israelites. The tenth and last plague caused the death of firstborn male children and animals.

2. Read Exodus 12:1-13, 21-23.

- What qualities did an animal have to have to be sacrificed? (*See verse 5.*)

- What did the Israelites do with this animal's blood? (*See verses 7 and 22.*)

- What sign caused God to pass over a home without sending the plague of death? (*See verses 12-13, 23.*)

- God told the Israelites to remember their deliverance from death. What was the name of this memorial? (*See verse 27.*)

ACTIVITY
Map: page 8. Draw a door with blood on three sides at Goshen.

Tell why this name describes God:
Merciful Protector

The Israelites Leave Egypt

15

Exodus 14:1-31

When Moses led the Israelites out of Egypt, God made a path through the Red Sea for the Israelites to continue toward Canaan, the promised land.

1. **Read Exodus 14:1-12.** Why did the boldness of the Israelites (in verse 8) change to fear (in verse 10)?

 **2.** **Read Exodus 14:1-2, 9.** What was the name of the place where the Israelites camped? Find this place on the map on page 8.

3. **Read Exodus 14:13-14.** What did Moses say that showed his faith in God?

4. **Read Exodus 14:15-31.** Look for three miraculous acts that God performed. God performed these miracles to help the Israelites escape from Egypt.

ACTIVITY
Map: page 8. Draw a path across the Red Sea near Pi Hahiroth.

Tell why this name describes God:
Merciful Protector

16 The Ten Commandments

Exodus 20:1-17

 In the wilderness between Egypt and Canaan, God, the Holy One, gave the Israelites a set of laws. These laws showed He hated sin.

1. **God gave a complete system of laws** to the nation of Israel. The central part was called the Ten Commandments. Read Exodus 20:1-7. Name each law in two to four words.

   ① _____ ⑥ _____

   ② _____ ⑦ _____

   ③ _____ ⑧ _____

   ④ _____ ⑨ _____

   ⑤ _____ ⑩ _____

2. **What do these laws tell us** about who God is and what He is like?

3. **In your country,** which of these laws do people often break?

4. **What do these laws tell us** about what human beings are like?

5. **How many of God's laws** does a person have to break to be guilty of doing wrong— to have sinned? Think about Adam and Eve. *(See event 5 on page 16.)*

ACTIVITY
Map: page 8. Draw the two stone tablets near Mt. Sinai.

Tell why this name describes God:
Lawgiver with all Authority to make Laws

17 🌐 Tabernacle in the Wilderness

Exodus 40:17-34; Leviticus 1:1-4, 10

God then directed Moses to build a movable place for worship. There the Israelites offered sacrifices and received forgiveness of their sins.

1. **Read Exodus 40:17-34.** Compare what you read with the picture of the tabernacle on page 10. (In verse 20, the "Testimony" means the two tablets of stone with the Ten Commandments. In verse 22, the "table" was the Table of Bread.)

2. **The tabernacle was a place of worship.** It was also a place where a person's sin could be atoned (covered or forgiven) by offering a sacrifice from his herds of cattle and goats, from his flock of sheep, or from his birds. The animal that was sacrificed was a substitute for the person, and it would die so the person's sin was forgiven. Read Leviticus 1:1-4, 10-14. What did the people do?

3. **What is similar** between what was done here and what happened in events 8 and 14 (pages 19 and 25)?

ACTIVITY
Tabernacle diagram (page 10) and map (page 8): Draw a lamb outside the Tabernacle and in the Wilderness.

Tell why this name describes God:
Holy God

18 The Bronze Serpent

Numbers 21:4-9

On their way toward Canaan, the Israelites rebelled against God. God punished them with deadly serpent bites but then provided a way to cure their suffering.

1. **Read Numbers 21:4-9.** Find each of the following parts in the story. Print the verse numbers, that match the following parts of the story, beside the appropriate line.

   - Sin of unbelief and rebellion

   - Judgment

   - Confession

   - Prayer for deliverance

   - God's provision

   - Faith

   - Life

2. **What did an Israelite** have to do to be saved from death?

3. **Remember this event.** A very important teacher later on will mention this event in the Bible's unfolding story. This teacher will explain then why this event is so important.

ACTIVITY
Map: page 8. Draw a pole with a snake wrapped on it near Edom.

Tell why these names describe God:
Supreme Authority   Merciful Protector

29

19

2 Samuel 7:1-16

After the Israelites entered Canaan, God ruled them through judges and kings. God promised that King David's kingdom would last forever through a special person in his family.

 1. **Israel was ruled** in Canaan by several judges, then by a series of kings. David, the second king, was the greatest and godliest. Read 2 Samuel 7:1-7. What kind of "house" did David want to build for God? Note: David gathered materials and made plans for a magnificent temple in Jerusalem. His son, King Solomon, later built the temple.

2. **"House" sometimes means** a person's descendants (people born into the same family over years and years). Read 2 Samuel 7:11-13. What kind of "house" did God promise to set up for David?

3. **Read 2 Samuel 7:16.** How long does this "house" continue after the reign of King Solomon?

4. **Read Genesis 49:10.** What tribe was David from? Remember Israel's promise. *(See event 12 on page 23.)*

 **ACTIVITY**
Map: page 8. Draw a crown near Jerusalem.

Tell why this name describes God:
Faithful Promise Keeper

20 Coming Messiah Prophesied

Isaiah 7:14; 9:1-2, 6-7; 52:13—53:12

Throughout the Israelites' history, God inspired His prophets to tell ahead of time details about a special Israelite, King, and Savior who would be born at a future time.

1. **His birth: Read Isaiah 7:14.** The promised conqueror of Satan would be the offspring of the woman; the father was not mentioned. *(See event 7 on page 18.)* What is the connection between Genesis 3:15 and Isaiah 7:14?

2. **His birthplace: Read Micah 5:2.** How does this verse relate to the scepter promise in Genesis 49:10? *(See event 12 on page 23.)*

3. **His ministry in Galilee: Read Isaiah 9:1-2, 6.** This is near the Sea of Galilee.

4. **His death: Read Isaiah 52:13—53:12.** What bad things would be done to the man described here? What good things would happen from his suffering?

5. **His resurrection from death: Read Psalm 16:8-10.** What does verse 10 say will happen?

6. **His eternal kingdom: Read Isaiah 9:6-7.**

Tell why this name describes God:
Truth Revealer

The Birth of Jesus Christ

21

Matthew 1:1-2, 18-25; Luke 2:1-14

At God's chosen time, He sent His Son to Earth. God's Son was born of a virgin named Mary. He would become the Special King and Savior God had promised for centuries.

1. Read Matthew 1:1-2. This is the beginning of the genealogy of Jesus. It lists the ancestors of Jesus. What do you remember about these ancestors?

- Abraham? *(See event 11.)*
- Isaac? *(See event 12.)*
- Jacob? *(See event 12.)*
- Judah? *(See event 12, point 3; event 19, point 4; and event 20.)*

2. Read Matthew 1:18-25. Jesus was a unique child. He was different from us.

- It was not by Joseph, but by the Holy Spirit that Mary became pregnant with Jesus before she and Joseph were married.
- The names of Jesus mean something special:
  What does "Jesus" mean?
  What does "Immanuel" mean?

 **3.** Read Luke 2:1-7. Compare what happened in these verses with what Micah prophesied in Micah 5:2. *(See event 20.)* Why did Joseph have to go to Bethlehem?

ACTIVITY

At the bottom of pages 33 to 51 are words which describe Jesus. As you did for the names of God, tell why these names describe Jesus from what you have learned. **Map:** page 8. Draw a manger near Bethlehem.

Tell why this name describes God:
Faithful Promise Keeper

Temptations by Satan

22

Matthew 4:1-11

At the beginning of His ministry, Jesus was tested by Satan. Jesus resisted Satan's temptations by quoting statements from God's Word in the Old Testament.

1. **To show that Jesus** was God's special Son and sinless, God's Spirit led Jesus into the desert. While Jesus was there, Satan, the greatest tempter, tempted Jesus three times.

2. Read Matthew 4:1-4. What was the first temptation? How did Jesus answer Satan?

3. Read Matthew 4:5-7. What was the second temptation? How did Jesus answer Satan?

4. Read Matthew 4:8-11. What was the third temptation? How did Jesus answer Satan?

5. **How is the way Jesus** responded to Satan's temptations different from how Eve responded to Satan's temptations? *(See event 5 on page 16.)*

ACTIVITY

Map: page 7. Draw a scroll in the desert above Jericho. This may have been where Jesus was tempted by Satan.

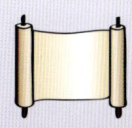

Tell why this name describes Jesus:
Satan Conqueror

23

John 1:29-34

God's prophet, John the Baptist, announced that Jesus of Nazareth was the Special King and Savior. He was God's Lamb, who would take away the sin of the world.

 **1.** **Jesus grew up in Nazareth.** Joseph, His earthly father, worked there as a carpenter.

 **2.** **When Jesus was about 30 years old,** He began teaching and healing people. At that time, there was a popular prophet named John (John the Baptist) who was preaching that the Messiah was coming. He was also baptizing people in the Jordan River when they repented of their sin.

3. **Read John 1:29.** Do you remember what you studied about sacrificial lambs taking away sin? (*See event 17 on page 28.*) What do you think John meant when he saw Jesus and said, "Look, the Lamb of God"?

4. **Read John 1:30-34.** What other special things about Jesus can you find in these verses?

ACTIVITY
Map: page 7. Draw a hammer beside Nazareth. Draw a stick figure on the Jordan River.

Tell why these names describe Jesus:
Humble Human Being   Worshipped Lamb of God

24

Meeting with a Religious Leader

John 3:1-18

One time, Jesus told an important religious leader that he must experience a spiritual birth in order to enter God's kingdom.

1. Read John 3:1-4. What did Nicodemus think Jesus meant when He talked about being "born again"?

2. Read John 3:5-8. What kind of rebirth was Jesus talking about?

3. **What do you think** Jesus meant when He talked about the need to be born again by the Spirit? Hint: Read John 1:10-13. "He" refers to Jesus.

4. **Review what happened to the Israelites** with the bronze serpent in Numbers 21:4-9. (See event 18 on page 29.) Now read John 3:14. Note: Son of Man is a common title for Jesus. Based on what happened to the Israelites, what do you think Jesus was predicting would happen to Him?

5. Read John 3:15-18. What is the main idea in these verses?

Meeting with a Samaritan Woman

25

John 4:3-42
Another time, Jesus explained to a woman in Samaria how God could permanently satisfy her spiritual thirst.

1. **In Jesus' day,** most Jewish people thought they were much better than people from Samaria. Some Jews even hated the Samaritans. Religious leaders did not allow Jews to speak to these people because they thought the Samaritans were religiously unclean. Read John 4:3-9.

2. **Read John 4:10-15.** What kind of water was the woman thinking about? How was that water different from the "water" Jesus was talking about?

3. **Read John 4:16-18.** What do we learn in these verses about this woman?

4. **Read John 4:19-26.** What did Jesus tell the woman about Himself?

5. **Read John 4:28-29.** How did Jesus know so much about this woman?

6. **Read John 4:30, 39-42.** How did other Samaritans respond to Jesus? What did they decide to believe?

Tell why this name describes Jesus:
Truth Revealer

26 Jesus Claims Oneness with God

John 5:16-23; 8:48-59; 10:22-33

Several times when Jesus declared that He was equal to and one with God, some people were greatly offended and tried to kill Him.

1. **The Jews believed** that if an ordinary man claimed to be God or equal to God, that man committed the sin of blasphemy. The punishment for blasphemy was death by stoning.

2. **Read John 5:16-23.** *True or False? Circle one.*

> **When Jesus claimed that God was His Father, He was saying that He had the same and equal nature as God.**

3. **Read John 8:48-59.** In event 1, we learned God is eternal or everlasting and has no beginning or end. What did Jesus reveal about Himself in these verses? Now read Exodus 3:14 and compare it with John 8:48-59. *(See event 13 on page 24.)*

4. **Read John 10:22-33.** Were the Jews correct when they thought that Jesus was claiming to be God?

Teachings about Hell

**Mark 9:42-48;
Luke 16:19-31**

As Jesus moved among people, He warned them that eternal punishment in Hell was real. He told them they needed to escape it immediately. He said this sternly, but also lovingly.

1. **In an earlier event,** we learned that God created an everlasting fire to punish the Devil and his angels. *(See event 4 on page 15.)* Read Matthew 25:41. Jesus warned those who follow Satan that they will experience the same eternal punishment.

2. **Read Mark 9:42-48.** What phrase did Jesus use in verse 48 to describe what Hell is like?

3. **Jesus once told** about a man who died and went to Hell (Hades). Read Luke 16:19-31. What did Jesus teach about Hell?

   - *True or False? Circle one.*

     Hell is a place where people constantly know they are suffering.

   - *True or False? Circle one.*

     Once people are in Hell, they can escape.

Tell why these names describe Jesus:
Authoritative Teacher   Truth Revealer

28 Miracles of Jesus

Matthew 4:23-24; John 11:1-45

Jesus healed sick and disabled people. He cast out demons and raised people from the dead. He did this to show His compassion for people who suffered and to show His divine power.

1. **Jesus performed many miracles** to show that He was "the Son of God," as John the Baptist had said.

2. **Read Matthew 4:23-24.** What kinds of miracles did Jesus perform as He went throughout the region of Galilee and ministered to people?

3. **Read John 11:1-4.** According to Jesus, what was the reason for Lazarus' sickness?

4. **Read John 11:5-16.** What did Jesus know that His disciples did not know?

5. **Read John 11:17-27.** What did Jesus tell Martha about Himself? What did He ask her? How did Martha answer?

6. **Read John 11:28-45.** Look carefully at verses 40-45. Many of the Jews saw this miracle which Jesus did. How did they respond?

Note: Jews in the New Testament descended from the Israelites of the Old Testament.

Tell why this name describes Jesus:
Miracle Worker

29

Jesus Is Betrayed

Matthew 26:1-2, 14-28, 45-56

When Judas Iscariot (one of Jesus' 12 disciples) betrayed Him, Jesus did not supernaturally resist arrest. He willingly submitted Himself to His captors.

1. **Before you read** from Matthew 26, read the prophecy in Psalm 41:7-9.

2. **Read Matthew 26:1-2.** What did Jesus know would happen to Him?

3. **Read Matthew 26:14-28.** Jesus predicted that His captors would break His body and shed His blood. How does Jesus' statement, in verse 28, help us understand what John the Baptist said earlier, when he proclaimed, "Behold! The Lamb of God who takes away the sin of the world!"? *(See event 22 on page 33.)*

4. **Read Matthew 26:45-56.** Did Jesus have the power to resist arrest? Why do you think that He willingly allowed Himself to be arrested?

Tell why this name describes Jesus:
Willing Substitute

30

Matthew 27:1-2, 11-24

Jesus was never proven guilty of any wrongdoing in any religious or civil court. He was unjustly beaten and condemned to die by Roman crucifixion.

1. **Read Matthew 27:1-2.** What do we see in these verses that indicate Jesus would not receive a fair trial?

2. **Read Matthew 27:11-14.** Did Jesus deny the accusation that He was the King of the Jews?
   - • In Genesis 49:10, God promised that the scepter, a sign of royalty, would not depart from the tribe of Judah. As a descendant of Judah, Jesus was able to be the Jewish King. Review point 3 in event 12 on page 23.
   - • Review points 2, 3, and 4 in event 19 on page 30. As a descendant of King David, who was also from the tribe of Judah, Jesus was able to reestablish the royal reign of King David's family.

3. **Read Matthew 27:15-24.** What statements in these verses indicate that Jesus was not guilty of the crimes for which He was tried?

Tell why these names describe Jesus:
Sinless Man   Rejected Messiah   Israel's Promised King

31

**Luke 23:26-38;
1 Corinthians 5:7**

Jesus then died on a cross as the perfect sacrificial Lamb for our sins. His death crushed Satan's head, just as God had promised to Adam and Eve.

1. **The Jewish historian** Josephus described crucifixion as "the worst kind of death." First, a prisoner was beaten cruelly with a short, heavy whip. Then he was nailed to a cross where he suffered terrible pain and shame for hours before he died.

2. **Read Psalm 22:1-18.** King David wrote this psalm about the Jewish Messiah 1,000 years before Jesus was born and hundreds of years before crucifixion was used as a death penalty in Canaan. Look for statements that show the man described in this psalm (the Messiah) would die by crucifixion.

3. **Read Luke 23:26-38.** What does Jesus' prayer in verse 34 tell us about Him?

4. **Read the last phrase** in 1 Corinthians 5:7. What was similar between the Passover lambs that were killed in Egypt and Jesus' death on the cross? *(See event 14 on page 25.)*

ACTIVITY
Map: page 7. Draw a cross at Jerusalem.

Tell why these names describe Jesus:
Willing Substitute   Perfect Sacrifice

32 A Repentant, Dying Thief

Luke 23:39-47

As Jesus was dying, one guilty man, who was crucified beside Him, placed his faith in Jesus and received the gift of life in a place of paradise after he died.

1. **Read Luke 23:39-42.** Which of these were true of the criminal who repented?

◯ He feared God.

◯ He acknowledged his own guilt.

◯ He acknowledged Jesus' innocence.

◯ He believed that Jesus was truly a king.

◯ He believed in life beyond death.

◯ He believed that Jesus could give him some kind of "kingdom favor."

◯ He made a simple request of Jesus because he had faith in Him.

2. **Read Luke 23:43.** What was Jesus' promise? When did He give the promise? How certain is the promise?

3. **What other paradise** did God provide much earlier in the Bible? *(See event 3 on page 14.)*

4. **Read Luke 23:44-47.** What did the Roman centurion decide about Jesus?

5. **Read Mark 15:33-39.** What other historical facts are given about Jesus' death?

Tell why this name describes Jesus:
Sin Forgiver

33

Resurrection of Jesus

Luke 24:1-12, 36-43

On the third day after Jesus died and was buried, God supernaturally raised Him from the dead to show His power over sin, death, and Hell.

1. Read Hebrews 2:14-15.

- What was the purpose for Jesus' death in verse 14?

- In verse 15?

2. Read Luke 24:1-12. What verses show that Jesus was no longer in the tomb?

3. Read Luke 24:36-43. What did Jesus do to prove that He was not just a spirit and that His physical body had been raised from the dead?

4. **Because God raised Jesus** from the dead, are these statements *True or False?*

- *T or F: We can have confidence that what Jesus said about Himself was true.*

- *T or F: We can have confidence that God was satisfied with Jesus' death as a payment for our sins.*

5. **As you think about** what we have studied, how would you answer this question: Who is Jesus? One great literary critic and philosopher has said that there are only three possible answers:

☐ He was a lunatic.   ☐ He was a liar.   ☐ He was and is the Lord as He said.

Tell why this name describes Jesus:
Resurrected Savior

34 Ascension of Jesus

1 Corinthians 15:3-8; Acts 1:6-11

After His resurrection, Jesus appeared many times to His disciples on earth. Then He ascended to Heaven to be with His Father.

1. Read 1 Corinthians 15:3-8. *True or False? Circle one.*

More than 500 people saw Jesus alive after His resurrection. Most of them were still living when Paul wrote this letter to the Corinthians.

2. Read Acts 1:6-8. Verse 8 records the last words Jesus spoke on earth. Summarize what Jesus said to His followers.

3. Read Acts 1:9-11. What promise did the two men (angels) give to the followers of Jesus?

4. A few chapters later in Acts, Jesus appears another time in the story of the Bible. Read Acts 7:54-56. Where was Jesus at that time?

5. What is Jesus doing now in Heaven? Read Hebrews 7:24-25. Hint: The words "He" and "Him" (that appear in most versions of the Bible) refer to Jesus.

ACTIVITY
Map: page 7. Draw a cloud beside the Mt. of Olives.

Tell why this name describes Jesus:
Ascended Son of God

35 Peter Proclaims the Good News

Acts 2:22-36

Soon after Jesus ascended, His disciples began to proclaim the good news about who Jesus was, what He did, and why people should trust in Him as their Savior.

1. **Ten days after Jesus ascended to Heaven,** the Holy Spirit of God came upon the followers of Jesus, just as He had promised.

2. **With the power of God's Spirit** upon him, Simon Peter (one of Jesus' disciples) spoke his first message about Jesus. What did Peter say about Jesus from what he personally had seen and heard? Read Acts 2:22-35.

- His Life. *(See verse 22.)*

- His Death. *(See verse 23.)*

- His Resurrection. *(See verses 24-32.)* Peter quoted Psalm 16:8-10 in verses 25-28. King David wrote this psalm 1,000 years before Jesus lived on earth.

- His Ascension. *(See verses 33-35.)*

3. **What did Peter** conclude about Jesus of Nazareth? Read verse 36.

Tell why these names describe Jesus:
Miracle Worker   Resurrected Savior   Ascended Son of God

36 Jesus' Return for Believers

**John 14:1-3;
1 Thessalonians
4:13-18**

Just as He promised during His earthly ministry, Jesus will return to take those who have truly believed in Him to be with Him in a heavenly paradise.

1. **The final five events** in this short version of *The Story of Hope* have not happened yet. This event is the first of those five events. Up until now, we have studied Bible history. But now we will see how the Bible moves from Bible history (past events) to Bible prophecy (future events).

2. **Before His death,** what did Jesus tell His disciples to comfort them? Read John 14:1-3.

3. **To learn more** about this return of Jesus for believers (that we call "the rapture"), read 1 Thessalonians 4:13-18.

   ■ What will happen to Jesus' followers who have already died?

   ■ What will happen to Jesus' followers who are still alive when He returns?

4. **Read 1 Corinthians 15:51-57.** What else do these verses say about the return of Jesus?

Jesus' Return as King

37

Revelation 19:11-19; 20:1-6

Soon after His return for believers, Jesus will come back with those He took to Heaven and will reign as King over the whole earth.

1. **The book of Revelation** is written in a way that uses many symbols to explain what is going to happen in the future. As we understand what the symbolic words mean, we can see four major facts. Read Revelation 19:11-19.

- Jesus will return to the earth. (How do we know this is the Jesus we have studied?)

- Jesus will be accompanied by the armies of Heaven. (Who will be in these armies?)

- Jesus then will defeat those who oppose Him. (Who are these enemies of Jesus?)

- When Jesus defeats His enemies, God will be just in carrying out His wrath on them. (Why is this judgment just and fair?)

2. **Read Revelation 20:1-3.** Who is the "old serpent" and what will happen to him? *(See events 4, 5, and 7.)*

3. **Read Revelation 20:4-6.** What will take place on the earth for 1,000 years? Throughout the Bible it is predicted that Jesus will reign as a king sometime in the future. *(See events 12, 19, 21, 30, and 34.)*

Tell why this name describes Jesus:
Satan Conqueror

38

Satan's Final Destiny

Revelation 20:7-10

Near the end of Jesus' kingdom, Satan will make a final attempt to lead a rebellion against God. But Satan will fail, and God will throw him into the lake of fire that God prepared earlier for him.

1. **Before his final punishment,** Satan will be bound for a period of 1,000 years. Read Revelation 20:1-3.

2. **At the end of the 1,000 years,** Satan will be released temporarily. What will Satan do at that time? Read Revelation 20:7-9.

3. **Read and review Isaiah 14:15 and Matthew 25:41.** Read Revelation 20:10. What do we learn here about Satan's final punishment? *(See event 4 on page 15.)*

4. **Read and review Genesis 3:15.** What is the connection between Genesis 3:15 (in the third chapter of the Bible) and the final destiny of Satan described here (in the third chapter from the end of the Bible)? *(See event 7 on page 18.)*

Tell why this name describes Jesus:
Satan Conqueror

39

Revelation 20:11-15

Then at the end of earthly time, unbelievers will stand in front of God to be sentenced to eternal punishment for their sins.

1. **As this event begins,** what will happen to the Earth and Heaven that now exist? Read Revelation 20:11 and compare it with 2 Peter 3:10.

2. **Who do you think** will be the Judge on this great white throne? Read Revelation 20:11-12a (first phrase of verse 12).

3. **Books will play important roles** when unbelievers stand before the Judge at this "Great White Throne Judgment." Read Revelation 20:12-13.

- What will unbelievers be judged for from "the books"?

- What was written in "the Book of Life"?

4. **Read Revelation 20:14-15.** Who will be cast into the lake of fire?

- According to verse 14?

- According to verse 15?

Tell why this name describes God:
Just Judge

Joyful Destiny for Believers

40

Revelation 21:1—22:5

But God's story ends with wonderful news. Everyone who has trusted Jesus as his or her Savior will enter a beautiful paradise where there is no sin and they will live there eternally with God.

1. **How will believers** enjoy God's eternal paradise? Read Revelation 21:1-3.
   - They will go up to Heaven to enjoy paradise, or ...
   - God will bring paradise down for them.

2. **Read Revelation 21:4—22:5** to learn more about this eternal paradise.
   - Who is "the Lamb"? *(See verse 14.)*
   - What will not be found in the new, holy city?
   - What are some of the most spectacular features of this new city?
   - Who will be allowed to live in this new paradise? Read Revelation 21:27.

3. **How long** will they live there? Read Revelation 22:5.

4. **Do you think that your name** is written in the Lamb's Book of Life? Check One.
   - ⬭ Yes ⬭ No ⬭ Not sure *What are the reasons for your answer?*

Tell why this name describes God:
Worshipped Lamb of God

51

God
What we have learned about our Creator:

☑ **Check the box beside each point you understand.**

The Bible says:

☐ He is eternal. This means He has always existed and will exist forever.

☐ He is holy. He is without sin at all.

☐ He is the creator who created the world and everything in it.

☐ He is all-powerful.

☐ He gave people commands to obey.

☐ He is a fair Judge and must punish disobedience.

Do you believe what the Bible teaches about God?

☐ YES

☐ NO

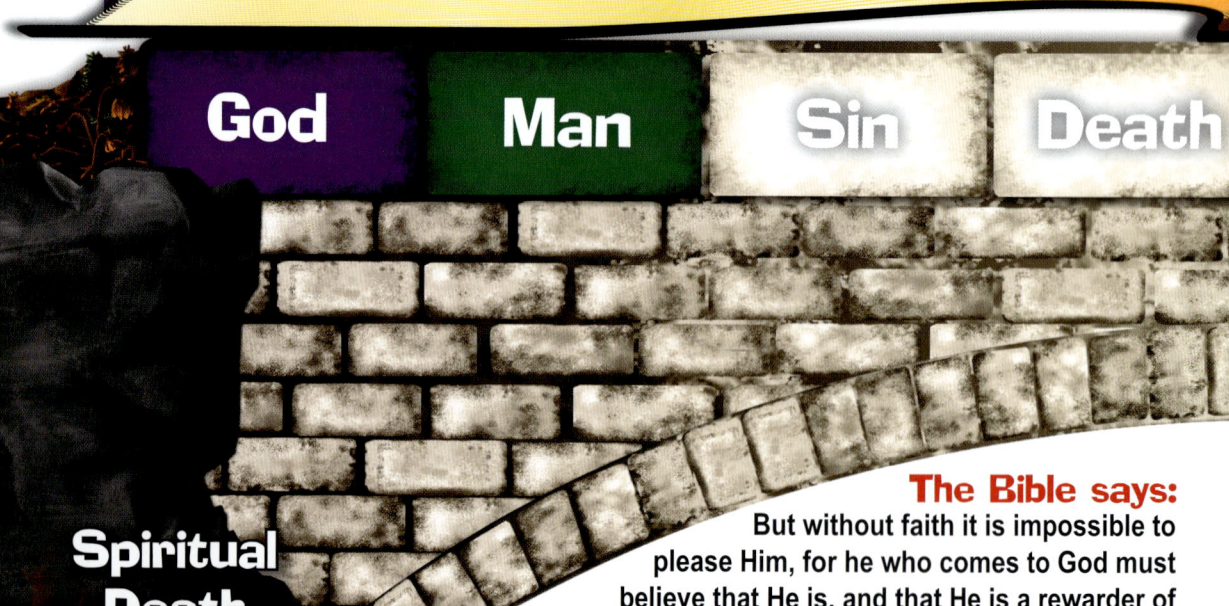

God   Man   Sin   Death

Spiritual Death

The Bible says:
But without faith it is impossible to please Him, for he who comes to God must believe that He is, and that He is a rewarder of those who diligently seek Him. *(Hebrews 11:6)*

Man

What we have learned about human beings:

☑ **Check the box beside each point you understand.**

The Bible tells us:

- ☐ We are made by God.
- ☐ God loves us and wants us to enjoy Him.
- ☐ God gives us the responsibility to obey Him.
- ☐ He also made us so that we can choose to disobey.
- ☐ God deserves that we obey Him completely.
- ☐ He loves us even when we disobey Him.

Do you believe what the Bible teaches about Man?

☐ **YES**

☐ **NO**

Christ   Cross   Faith   Life

Eternal Life

The Bible says:

And the LORD God formed man of the dust of the ground, and breathed into his nostrils the breath of life: and man became a living being. (Genesis 2:7)

EIGHT IMPORTANT TRUTHS FROM

Sin

What we have learned about disobedience to God:

☑ **Check the box beside each point you understand.**

The Bible says:

☐ God created, loved, and provided for Adam and Eve but they rebelled against Him.

☐ They disobeyed God when they ate from the one tree whose fruit He told them not to eat.

☐ Disobeying God is called *sin*.

☐ Adam and Eve's sin ruined their perfect relationship with God.

☐ Everyone inherited their sinful nature; all have sinned.

☐ God, who is a holy and just Judge, must punish sin.

☐ The punishment for sin is death.

Do you believe what the Bible teaches about Sin?

☐ YES

☐ NO

God **Man** **Sin** **Death**

Spiritual Death

The Bible says:

For all have sinned and fall short of the glory of God.
(Romans 3:23)

Death

What we have learned about the penalty for sin:

☑ **Check the box beside each point you understand.**

The Bible tells us death separates.

○ Adam and Eve died *spiritually* (became separated from God) the moment they sinned. All people since Adam and Eve are born spiritually dead.

○ Adam and Eve died *physically* (when one's spirit separates from the body) as do all their descendants.

○ Physical death is not the end. After a person dies, he or she will appear before God, the just Judge.

○ People suffer eternal death and conscious punishment when they do not choose God's provision for sin.

Do you believe what the Bible teaches about Death?

○ YES

○ NO

Christ　　Cross　　Faith　　Life

Eternal Life

The Bible says:

And as it is appointed for men to die once, but after this the judgment. *(Hebrews 9:27)*

Christist

What we have learned about Jesus Christ:

☑ **Check the box beside each point you understand.**

The Bible says:

☐ After Adam and Eve sinned, God promised to send Someone who would conquer Satan.

☐ God kept His promise and sent His Son, Jesus, to rescue us from judgment.

☐ Jesus was born of a virgin named Mary.

☐ Jesus lived a completely perfect life and showed through His claims and miracles that He is God.

☐ Jesus is both God and man in one perfect person. He is truly unique and the only way to eternal life.

Do you believe what the Bible teaches about Christ?

☐ YES

☐ NO

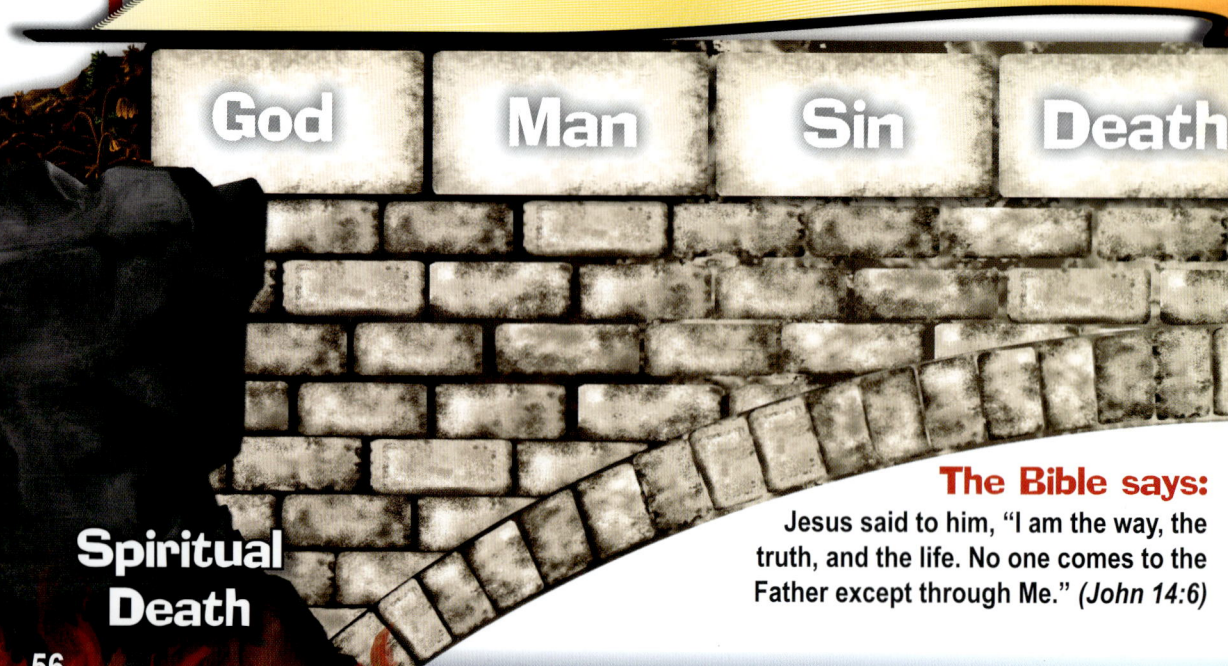

God Man Sin Death

Spiritual Death

The Bible says:

Jesus said to him, "I am the way, the truth, and the life. No one comes to the Father except through Me." *(John 14:6)*

Cross

What we have learned about Christ's death and resurrection:

☑ **Check the box beside each point you understand.**

The Bible tells us:

☐ God loves us even when we sin and provides the only way for us to be forgiven.

☐ In the Old Testament, God established sacrifices so sinners could have their sins forgiven.

☐ Then God sent His Son, Jesus, to be the one perfect and final sacrifice for sin.

☐ Jesus willingly died in our place, for our sins, on a cross, to rescue us from death and give us eternal life.

☐ Three days later, Jesus rose from the dead showing God accepted Jesus' sacrifice as payment for our sins.

Do you believe what the Bible teaches about the Cross?

☐ YES

☐ NO

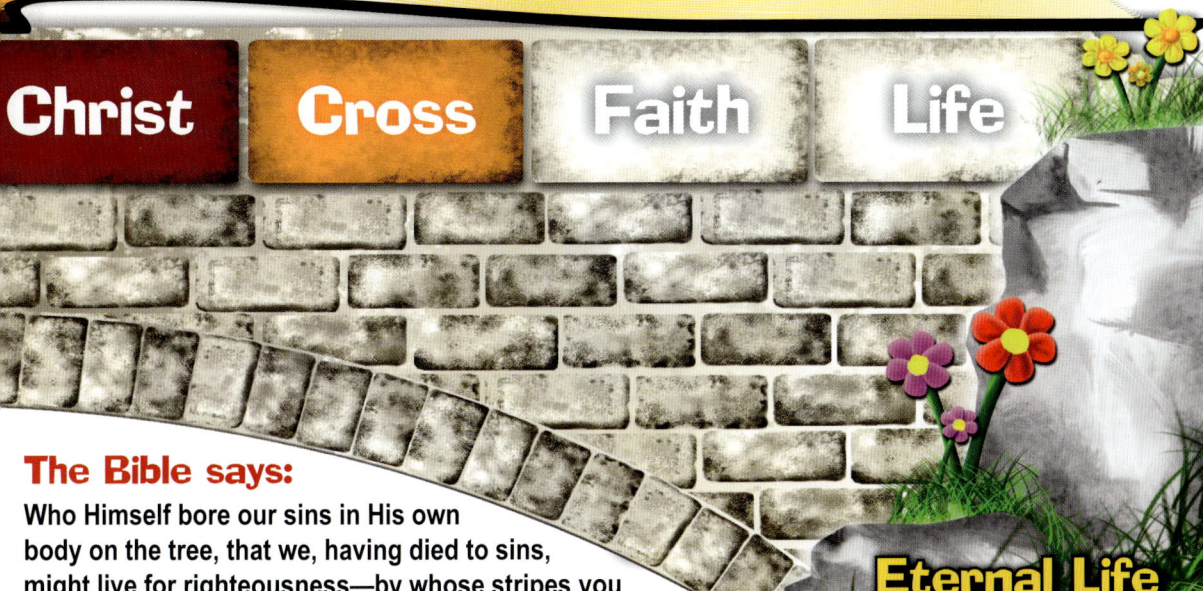

Christ **Cross** Faith Life

Eternal Life

The Bible says:

Who Himself bore our sins in His own body on the tree, that we, having died to sins, might live for righteousness—by whose stripes you were healed. *(1 Peter 2:24)*

Faith What we have learned about trusting Jesus Christ:

☑ **Check the box beside each point you understand.**

The Bible says:

☐ The Gospel of Jesus Christ offers eternal salvation that does not require people to work for or earn it.

☐ No sinful human being could ever earn salvation.

☐ God provided the way to pay our punishment for sin through the death of His Son Jesus.

☐ Because Jesus was punished for sin instead of us, God offers salvation to us as a free gift.

☐ God promises to forgive us if we repent (quit trusting the good things we do) and believe (trust) in His Son, Jesus Christ, alone to save us.

Do you believe what the Bible teaches about Faith?

☐ YES

☐ NO

God **Man** **Sin** **Death**

Spiritual Death

The Bible says:
For by grace you have been saved through faith, and that not of yourselves; it is the gift of God, not of works, lest anyone should boast. *(Ephesians 2:8-9)*

Life
What we have learned about eternal life:

☑ **Check the box beside each point you understand.**

The Bible tells us:

☐ When we repent and trust in Jesus, we pass from spiritual death to spiritual life.

☐ This new spiritual life God gives is eternal and will never be taken from us.

☐ We have new desires and want to love, obey, worship, and serve God from our hearts.

☐ We know our names are recorded in the Lamb's Book of Life and when we die we go into God's presence.

☐ There we will enjoy life eternally in a beautiful, sinless, pain-free paradise on a perfectly restored new Earth.

Do you believe what the Bible teaches about Life?

☐ YES

☐ NO

Christ **Cross** **Faith** **Life**

Eternal Life

The Bible says:
Jesus said to her, "I am the resurrection and the life. He who believes in Me, though he may die, he shall live. And whoever lives and believes in Me shall never die." *(John 11:25-26)*

My Personal Faith Response

▶ **Read the following words of Jesus.**

Instead of "the world," "whoever," and "he who," put in your name.

John 3:16-18

16 For God so loved **the world** that He gave His only begotten Son, that **whoever** believes in Him should not perish but have everlasting life. 17 For God did not send His Son into **the world** to condemn **the world**, but that **the world** through Him might be saved. 18 **He who** believes in Him is not condemned; but **he** who does not believe is condemned already, because **he** has not believed in the name of the only begotten Son of God.

I now understand that the God of the Bible is the One True God.
He is perfect and holy.

I now see myself much differently than I did before because of what I have learned from what the Bible teaches. I now understand that I was born with a sinful nature. I have disobeyed God continually. My sin grieves God very much even though He made me and loves me. I know my sin has separated me from God. The right (just) punishment for my sin is to be separated from God eternally in Hell, a place the Bible says is full of torment.

I understand that the death and resurrection of God's Son Jesus Christ is the only way for me to be forgiven, to escape the punishment for my sins, and to receive God's gift of eternal life.

I am now trusting Jesus Christ and His death on the cross and no one or nothing else as the only way God can forgive my sin.

It would be good now to tell God that you believe the statements above and are trusting what Jesus Christ did for you.

NEXT
STEPS
with Jesus

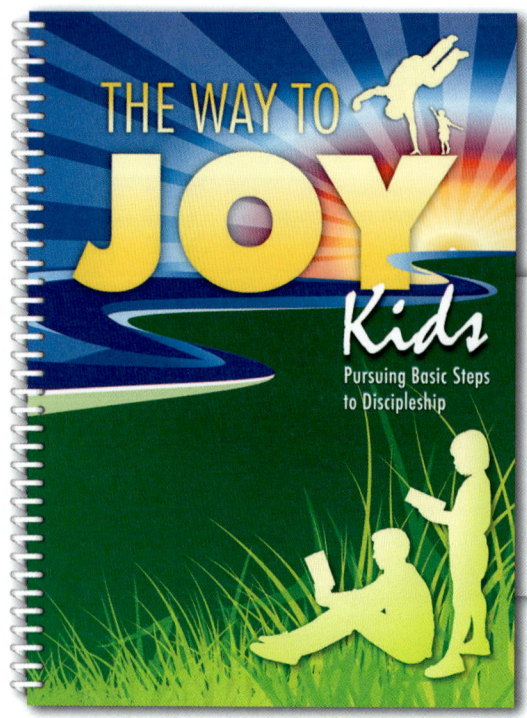

The Way to Joy – Kids
Pursuing Basic Steps to Discipleship

A basic discipleship study workbook for kids, ages 8-12. Ten lessons, with an accompanying Bible reading and prayer journal. 64 pages, plastic-coil binding.

$8.00 Each

5-9 Books	**$7** each
10-49 Books	**$6** each
50-99 Books	**$5** each
100+ Books	**$4** each

Free Downloadable
* Leader's Guide (for individual studies)

www.GoodSoil.com/free

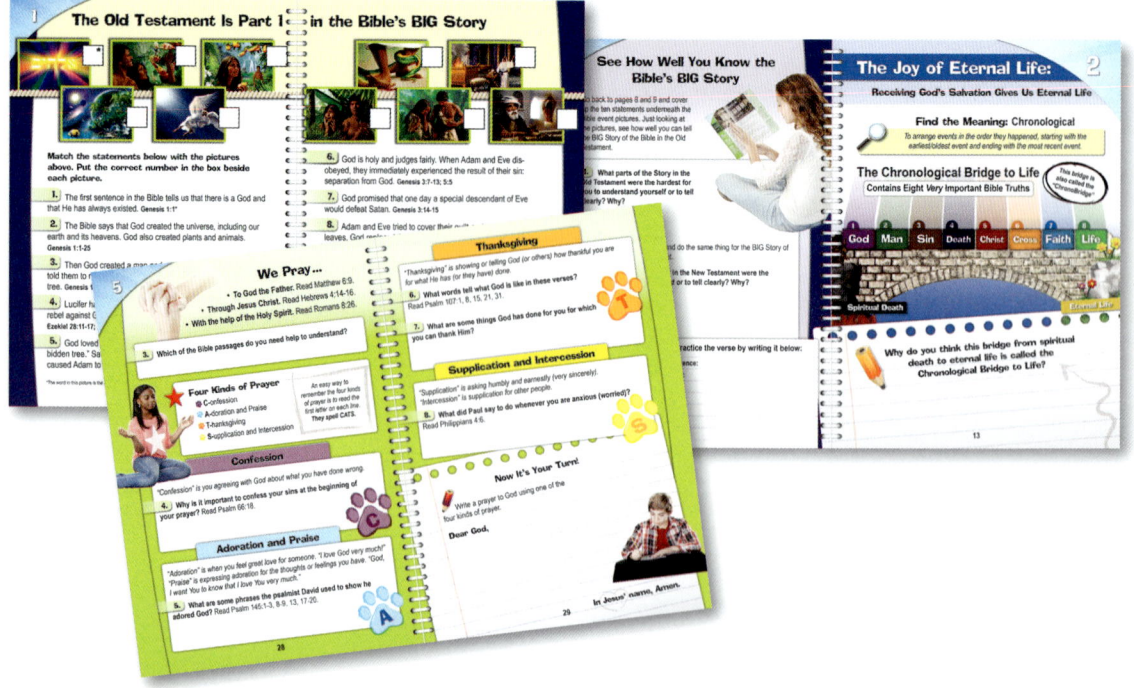

Adventures in The Story of Hope
Curriculum for Teaching God's Redemptive Story

This FREE curriculum guide includes 40 complete lesson plans and activities for teaching the Bible's BIG story of redemption, from Genesis through Revelation, to kids ages 8 through 12 years old.

The curriculum contains a variety of teaching aids and activities and is FREE for you to download. But there are other Good Soil Evangelism and Discipleship supplemental for-purchase resources that you may want to use with the curriculum:

- **The Story of Hope—Kids**
- **The Way to Joy—Kids**
- **The Bible's BIG Story PowerPoint CD**
- **The Bible's BIG Story Teaching Visuals**
- **Kids Sing the Story of Hope CD**
- **Kids Worship the God of the Big Story CD**
- **The Chronological Bridge to Life Cards and Visuals**

➡ **Free Download**
www.GoodSoil.com/free

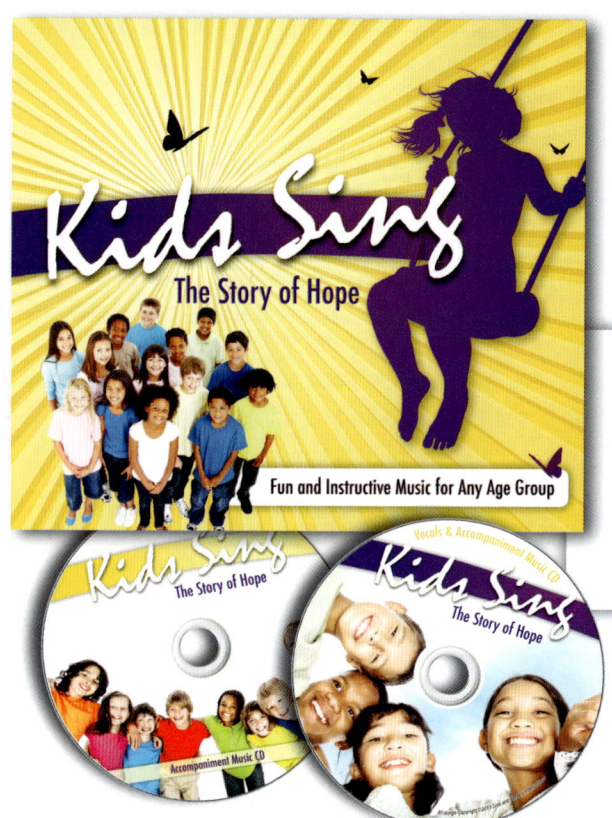

Kids Sing
The Story of Hope
Fun & Instructive Music for All Ages

Twelve kids-tested songs for learning and reviewing some of the key events in **The Story of Hope**. CD 1 includes the 12 songs sung by an ensemble of kids and their adult leaders. CD 2 is an instrumental-only recording of the soundtrack.

$20.00 Each
2 or more   **$16** each

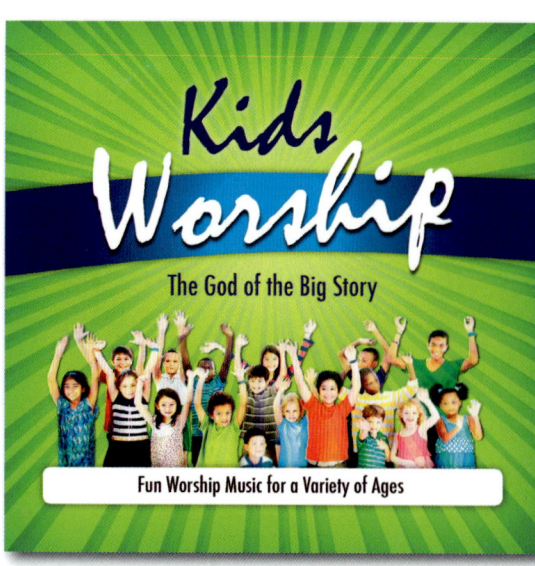

Kids Worship
The God of the Big Story
Worship Music for a Variety of Ages

Twelve worship-focused songs, including The God of the Big Story, Transcendent God, Doxology 21, We Believe, Tell the World of Jesus, and others. The songs are sung by an ensemble of kids and their adult leaders.

$10.00 Each
2 or more   **$8** each